THE LEGEND OF THE
WHITE BUFFALO WOMAN

W9-BTQ-984

Books by Paul Goble

Red Hawk's Account of Custer's Last Battle
Brave Eagle's Account of the Fetterman Fight
Lone Bull's Horse Raid
The Friendly Wolf
The Girl Who Loved Wild Horses
The Gift of the Sacred Dog
Star Boy
Buffalo Woman
The Great Race of the Birds and Animals
Death of the Iron Horse
Her Seven Brothers
Beyond the Ridge
Dream Wolf
I Sing for the Animals
Crow Chief
Love Flute
The Lost Children
Adopted by the Eagles
The Return of the Buffaloes
Remaking the Earth
Iktomi and the Boulder
Iktomi and the Berries
Iktomi and the Ducks
Iktomi and the Buffalo Skull
Iktomi and the Buzzard
Hau Kola, Hello Friend
(Autobiography for children)

THE LEGEND OF THE WHITE BUFFALO WOMAN

Paul Goble

NATIONAL
GEOGRAPHIC
KiDS

Washington, D.C.

Copyright © 1998 Paul Goble

First paperback edition 2002

Published by National Geographic Partners, LLC. All rights reserved.
Reproduction of the whole or any part of the contents without written
permission from the publisher is prohibited.

Library of Congress Cataloging-in-Publication Data
Goble, Paul.
    The legend of the white buffalo woman / Paul Goble
        p. cm.
    Includes bibliographical references.
    Summary: A Lakota Indian legend in which the White Buffalo
Woman presents her people with the Sacred Calf Pipe,
which gives them the means to pray to the Great Spirit.
    ISBN 978-0-7922-7074-4 (hardcover)   ISBN 978-0-7922-6552-8 (paperback)
1. Indians of North America—Great Plains—Folklore. 2. Legends—
Great Plains. [1. Indians of North America—Great Plains—
Folklore. 2. Folklore—Great Plains.] I. Title.
E78.G73G67 1998
398.2'08997—dc21   97-24086   CIP

REFERENCES: *Primary:~* Joseph Epes Brown, **The Sacred Pipe:** Black Elk's Account of the Seven Rites of the Ogalala Sioux, (pp. 3-9), University of Oklahoma Press, Norman, 1953; John G. Neihardt, **Black Elk Speaks:** Being the Life Story of a Holy Man of the Ogalala Sioux, (pp. 3-5), William Morrow, New York, 1932; Frances Densmore, (Lone Man's account), **Teton Sioux Music,** (pp. 63-8), Bureau of American Ethnology, Washington, D.C., 1918.

Secondary:~ W. J. Bordeaux, **Conquering the Mighty Sioux,** (pp. 177-9), Sioux Falls, 1929; George Catlin, **Letters and Notes** on the Manners, Customs and Condition of the North American Indians, (Vol. 2, pp. 163-76), London, 1841; W. P. Clark, **The Indian Sign Language,** (pp. 89-90, 302-4), L. R. Hammersley, Philadelphia, 1885; Edward S. Curtis, **Prayer to the Great Mystery** the Uncollected Writing and Photography, (pp. 145-7), St. Martins Press, New York, 1995; George A. Dorsey, **Legend of the Teton Sioux Medicine Pipe,** (pp. 326-9), Journal of American Folk-Lore, Vol. XIX, No. 75, Chicago, 1906; Richard Erdoes, **Lame Deer,** Sioux Medicine Man, (pp. 247, 251-6), Davis Poynter, London, 1973; Royal B. Hassrick, **The Sioux:** Life and Customs of a Warrior Society, (pp. 257-60), University of Oklahoma Press, Norman, 1964; Thomas E. Mails, **Fools Crow,** (pp. 142-4), Doubleday, New York, 1979; Garrick Mallery, **Picture-Writing of the American Indians,** (pp. 290-1), Tenth Annual Report of the Bureau of Ethnology, Washington, D.C. , 1893; James Mooney, **The Ghost-Dance Religion** and the Sioux Outbreak of 1890, (pp. 297-8), Fourteenth Annual Report of the Bureau of Ethnology, Washington, D.C., 1896; Vivian One Feather, **Ehanni Ohunkakan,** (pp. 112-3), Red Cloud Indian School, Pine Ridge, 1974; Montana Lisle Reese, **Legends of the Mighty Sioux,** (pp. 45-6, 49-51), Fantab, Sioux Falls, 1941; J. L.Smith, **A Short History of the Sacred Calf Pipe of the Teton Dakota,** (pp. 1-3), University of South Dakota, Vermillion, 1967; R. D. Theisz, **Buckskin Tokens:** Contemporary Oral Narratives of the Lakota, (pp. 25-6), Sinte Gleska College, Rosebud, 1975; James R. Walker, **Lakota Belief and Ritual,** (pp. 109-11, 148-50), University of Nebraska Press, Lincoln, 1980; Clark Wissler, **Some Dakota Myths,** (202-3), Journal of American Folk-Lore, Vol XX, No 78, Chicago, 1907.

An anonymous collection of 32 typewritten myths and legends about Pipestone Quarry, Pipestone National Monument c. 1976.

Quotations: These will be found in the books listed above: *Chased by Bears,* Densmore (1918) p. 95; *Lame Deer,* Erdoes (1973) p. 251; *Nicholas Black Elk,* Neihardt (1932) p. 3; *Nicholas Black Elk,* Brown, (1953).

"Tunkasila, Oyate nipi kta ca, le camu"
That the Nation will live, I pray

Since 1888, the National Geographic Society has funded more than 12,000 research, exploration, and preservation projects
around the world. The Society receives funds from National Geographic Partners, LLC, funded in part by your purchase.
A portion of the proceeds from this book supports this vital work. To learn more, visit www.natgeo.com/info.

For more information, please call 1-800-647-5463 or write to the following address:

NATIONAL GEOGRAPHIC PARTNERS
1145 17th Street N.W.
Washington, D.C. 20036-4688, U.S.A.

www.nationalgeographic.com

National Geographic supports K–12 educators with ELA Common Core Resources.
Visit www.natgeoed.org/commoncore for more information.

Printed in China
16/RRDS/5

Author's Note

In this most important of all Lakota sacred legends, the Great Spirit gave the Sacred Calf Pipe so that people could pray and commune with him. He caused a white buffalo cow calf to be changed into a woman, who gave the pipe to the Sans Arcs Lakotas. It established the mystical relationship and love between people and buffaloes who lived together on the Great Plains.

Oral tradition does not tell when White Buffalo Woman gave the pipe, only that it was at a time of some great change or suffering caused by war or famine. White man's history suggests it might have been in the late 1600s when the Lakotas were driven out of Wisconsin and Minnesota by their neighbors who had obtained guns in trade, but this may be a too recent date.

With the pipe, White Buffalo Woman gave them back hope and direction, and a new way to pray. The Sacred Calf Pipe is thought of as the first pipe, every other pipe its child, blessed with its power and inviolability. There is a pipe at the center of the seven rites, and every ceremony. Primarily it is a person's means to be in communion with God.

I have taken the legend of the gift of the Sacred Calf Pipe and framed it with other related myths. I have not illustrated the Sacred Calf Pipe, of which no likeness should be made. The style of clothing illustrated is one which has been worn from about the 1870s, and which, with only small changes of fashion, is still worn by traditional dancers at powwows.

"Before talking of holy things we prepare ourselves by offerings. If two are to talk together, one will fill the pipe and hand it to the other, who will light it and offer it to the sky and earth. Then we will smoke together, and after smoking we will be ready to talk of holy things."

Chased by Bears (1912)

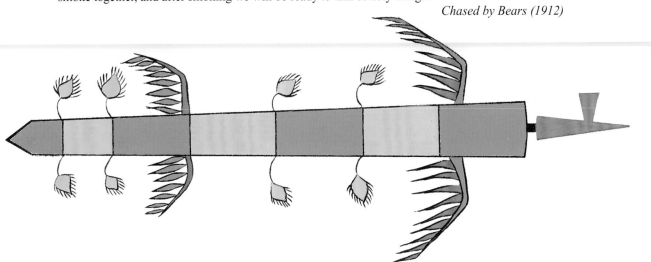

The pipe, above, is from a Lakota tipi cover (c. 1825) in the *Museum für Völkerkunde*, Berlin, Germany.
The pipe, opposite, is from a buffalo robe (c. 1845) in the Pitt Rivers Museum, Oxford, England.

End of the Old World

Long, long ago, the Great Spirit made it rain, day after day,
and the water rose, covering everything. The people climbed
a rocky ridge left jutting above the flood, yet even there
the water followed. And then the Four Winds blew, and huge
waves broke over the rocks and all the people were swept
away and drowned.

The Nation is Born Again

At the last moment an immense eagle swooped out of the sky to save a young woman who was crying for help. She clutched his feet, and he carried her to a faraway mountain which rose out of the water.

They married, and she gave birth to twins, a boy and a girl. From that marriage of a Woman of the Earth and the Eagle of the Sky, people had a new beginning, and in time grew to become a nation once more.

Sadness of War

Many generations passed, and then the people were attacked by enemies. Their houses were burned, and they were forced to leave their homeland in the forests. They fled to the great open plains, where there were no trees and where the Four Winds blew eternally across the circle of the world.

Every family mourned relatives who had been killed. Those were sad and frightening times.

White Buffalo Woman Appears

Late in the Spring of the year, a group of the people were wandering, strangers in the new country. They were tired and hungry, searching for the buffaloes.

Early one morning the leaders told two young men to climb a hill and look out over the country for the herds.

As they came to the top, they were surprised to see a young woman climbing up toward them on the other side, carrying a bundle on her back. She was a stranger, beautiful, and also mysterious.

One of the young men whispered bad thoughts, but his friend answered, "No! Get rid of such thoughts! She must be a holy woman." But he would not listen, and at the instant he put his arms round her, lightning flashed and thunder shook the hilltop, and rushing clouds hid them....

As the wind died, the clouds lifted, and the woman was standing there, alone. At her feet were bones which was all that was left of the foolish young man.

The other was so frightened he turned to run. "Stay!" she called, "No harm will come to you. Tell your leader I have something important to give him. Tell him to erect a council tipi with a buffalo skull altar at the center, and let everyone gather there at dawn tomorrow. Go now!"

He ran down to the camp as fast as he could, and told what had happened. They all wondered who this woman could be. The council tipi was set up just as she had asked.

Early the next morning everyone dressed in their best clothes and gathered inside the great tipi. They were excited, yet in awe of the Mysterious Woman.

As the sun lit up the sky, she appeared walking across the prairie toward the opening in the camp circle. Her breath was like a cloud in the cold morning air.

There was quiet. No baby cried; even the dogs feared to bark. She was singing, and though still far off her song was clearly heard:~
"With visible breath, I am walking,
Toward this Nation, I walk,
And my voice is heard as I walk.
With visible breath, I am walking,
With this red pipe, I walk."

The Beautiful Woman carried a pipe. She walked to the place of honor where the leader, Buffalo Standing Upright, invited her to sit. He dipped braided sweetgrass into a buffalo-horn cup filled with water for her to sip. "Sister, we are glad you have come," he said.

She thanked him, and she said to everyone, "Wakan Tanka, the Great Spirit, told my Buffalo People to send me to you today. He has seen your tears. He knows you have always tried to do what is right, so he gives you this pipe. Pray with it, and you will see your prayers rise up to him with the smoke, and you will know he hears you. The pipe will join nations and families together in love and peace, and so from today, your people and my Buffalo Nation will be one family."

The Beautiful One told them, "When you fill the pipe the spirits of all things will help you send your prayers to the Great Spirit."

She took a glowing chip from the fire and lit the pipe. She offered smoke to the Sky, and the Earth, and to the Four Winds, in thanks for all the good things which they give. She handed the pipe to the person on her left, and it went from hand to hand round the circle, and children touched it as it passed.

When the pipe had completed the circle she leaned it against the buffalo skull. She told them, "In time all of you will have a pipe. Carry it always, and the Great Spirit will help you on your pathway through life."

She said to Buffalo Standing Upright, "Look after this pipe,
and it will guide your people to the end of the world."

Turning to the people she said, "Pray always. Look for
what is good and true. And now I have finished what
I was sent to do. I will always remember you, and in time

I will return. *Mitakuye oyasin*—we are all related."

    She left the council tipi, stopping three times to turn and look back at them. When she had passed through the opening in the tipi circle, she turned a fourth time, and sat down.

And then everyone was amazed to see a white buffalo calf jump up and run off to join the buffalo herds. Until that moment nobody had noticed that the buffaloes surrounded the camp. The Wonderful Woman had brought her Buffalo Nation with her.

The Buffalo Path

She is called White Buffalo Woman because she changed into a white buffalo calf. Afterwards her Buffalo People gave the red stone so everyone could make pipes. It happened this way:~

Buffaloes made pathways as they walked from one grassland to another, this river to that, to and fro. At certain places the great beasts loved to lie down and roll in the dust or mud to scratch their backs! At one of those wallowing-places they uncovered the beautiful red stone. Walking the Buffalo Paths, people found it washed and polished by the wind and rain...a gift from the Buffalo People.

Blood Changed to Stone

Tradition tells that the red stone is the flesh and blood of the people who drowned at the end of the Old World. When the waves swept them off the high ridge, they sank, and the Great Spirit changed their bodies to stone.

*   *   *

*All these things, which have been told here, were born in the imagination of **Wakan Tanka**, the Great Spirit.*

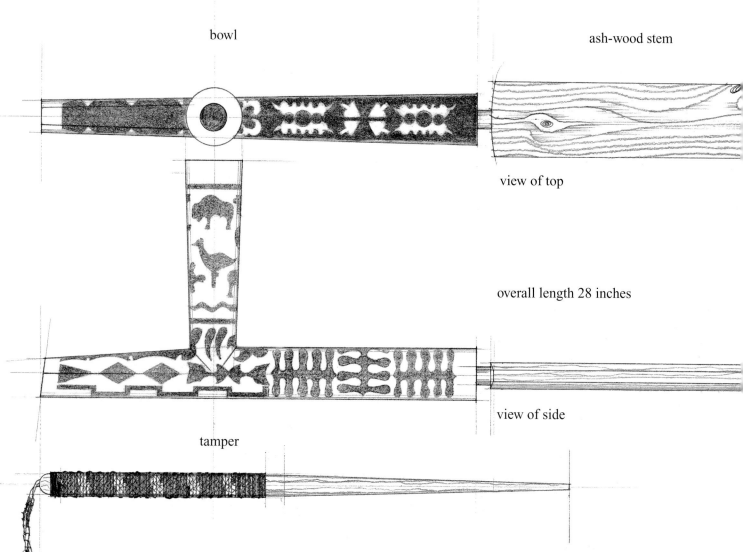

bowl

ash-wood stem

view of top

overall length 28 inches

view of side

tamper

Some Meanings of the Pipe

"If an Indian tries to talk about the pipe, he is easily lost. Our minds are not good enough to understand all of it." Lame Deer (1973)

Bowl is stone. It comes from the Earth, the *Mother* (material) and *Grandmother* (spiritual) of all, who give everything needful for life.

Stem is wood. It remembers the trees and plants. When pointing the stem upward we have our feet on Earth and our thoughts in the Sky, who is the *Father* (material) and *Grandfather* (spiritual) of all. The stem is straight like truth, and strong like the mind and concentration has to be. The hole through the middle is the soul.

Buffalo fur honors the animals and everything that walks and moves on Earth.

Mallard-duck feathers (green neck feathers) are for all who live in the water, for birds and everything that flies.

Four ribbons are the Four Winds:~
    black or **blue ribbon** is the *west* wind which brings the thunderstorms and rain, and *inspiration*.
    white ribbon is the *north* wind which brings snow in winter to purify the Earth, and to teach *endurance*.

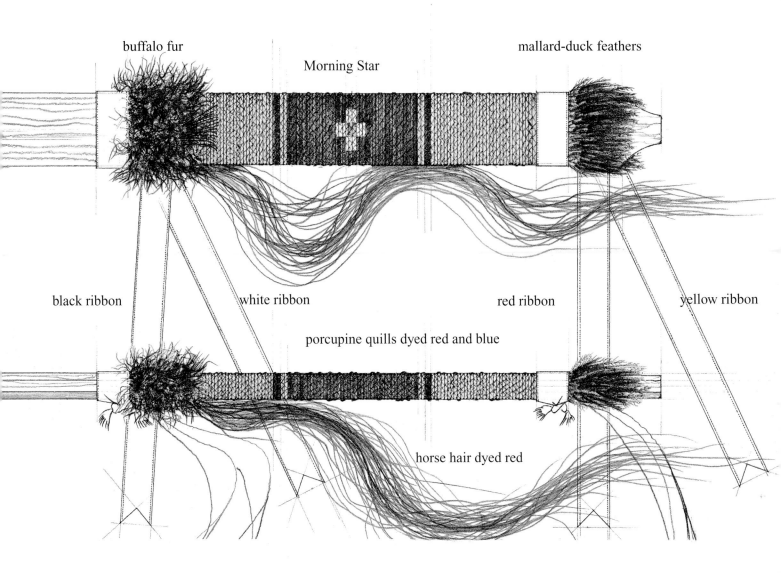

buffalo fur

Morning Star

mallard-duck feathers

black ribbon

white ribbon

red ribbon

yellow ribbon

porcupine quills dyed red and blue

horse hair dyed red

red ribbon is the *east* wind, the Sun and Morning Star who herald the new day in which we can look for *wisdom*.

yellow ribbon is the warm *south* wind which brings *life* and summertime. It is also the direction we will travel at *death*.

Tobacco grains remind us of the *abundance of God's blessings*.

When praying with the pipe, a person is at the central point where the powers of the six directions meet. Power flows from each, through the pipe, which is set alight with the *Fire*, the Great Spirit.

Tamper is for the *willpower* which we need in every endeavor.

*"And because it means all this, and more than any man can understand,
the pipe is holy."*   *Nicholas Black Elk (1932)*

The pipe illustrated was made for the author in 1986 by Myron Taylor, pipe-maker from Flandreau, South Dakota. The bowl is pipestone with lead inlay, and the stem is ash wood wrapped with porcupine quills.

■ **Pipestone Quarry** *is now a National Monument. In the old days it was a place of pilgrimage. People travelled great distances to quarry stone. Pipe bowls and unworked stone were traded across the continent. There was peace at the quarry, even between enemies, because tradition told it was the place where the Great Spirit had come down to Earth. Standing on the high ridge above the quarry, the same ridge from which the people had been swept by the waves, he told them to stop fighting, to smoke the pipe together and live in peace. Henry Wadsworth Longfellow captured the spirit of this story in his much-loved poem,* The Song of Hiawatha. *The pipe is often called the "peace-pipe."*

"Most people call it a 'peace pipe' yet now there is no peace on earth or even between neighbors. This is my prayer that through our sacred pipe peace may come to those people who can understand, an understanding which must be of the heart and not just of the head alone."

Nicholas Black Elk (1953)

One hundred and sixty years ago George Catlin, who travelled to paint Indian people, was one of the early white visitors to the quarry, and pipestone was named "Catlinite" after him. He recorded what Lakota people told him: ~

"This pipestone is part of our flesh. The red men are part of the red stone. If the white men take away a piece of the red pipestone, it is a hole in our flesh, and the blood will always run. We cannot stop the blood from running. The Great Spirit has told us that the red stone is only to be used for pipes, and through them we are to smoke to him. We love to go to the Pipestone Quarry, and get a piece of red stone for our pipes; but we ask the Great Spirit first."

Anonymous (1836)